Sacred Solitude: Embracing Celibacy for Spiritual Development

Copyright Page

TITLE: Sacred Solitude: Embracing Celibacy for Spiritual Development

1ST Edition

Copyright @ 2023

Roberto M. Rodriguez. All rights reserved.

ISBN: 9798223140276

Table of Contents

Sacred Solitude: Embracing Celibacy for Spiritual Development

By Roberto Miguel Rodriguez

Chapter 1: Understanding Celibacy for Spiritual Enlightenment

The Concept of Celibacy in Religion

Celibacy has long been a topic of intrigue and contemplation within religious communities. For Catholics, in particular, it holds a prominent place in the practice of faith. In this subchapter, we will explore the concept of celibacy in religion, and how it can be utilized for spiritual enlightenment, personal growth, self-discipline, activism, career focus, mental and emotional well-being, rebellion against societal expectations, cultivating a deeper connection with oneself, exploring alternative forms of intimacy, challenging traditional gender roles, and preserving personal energy and vitality.

For Catholics seeking spiritual enlightenment, celibacy offers a unique path to connect with the divine. By abstaining from sexual relationships, individuals can redirect their energy towards prayer, meditation, and contemplation. This intentional solitude allows for a deeper understanding of oneself and the spiritual truths that lie within.

Moreover, celibacy serves as a powerful tool for personal growth and self-discipline. By choosing to forego physical intimacy, individuals are challenged to develop a strong sense of self-control and mastery over their desires. This discipline extends beyond the realm of sexuality and can positively impact other areas of life, such as professional pursuits and personal relationships.

Celibacy can also be seen as a form of activism against societal pressures. By refusing to conform to societal expectations of relationships, individuals can challenge the notion that one's worth is determined solely by their ability to form romantic partnerships. This form of activism empowers individuals to prioritize their own personal goals and aspirations, rather than conforming to external pressures.

Furthermore, celibacy provides an opportunity to prioritize mental and emotional well-being. By removing the distractions and potential emotional turmoil that can arise from intimate relationships, individuals can focus on healing, self-care, and personal growth. This intentional solitude allows for the cultivation of a strong foundation of mental and emotional well-being.

Celibacy can also be seen as a form of rebellion against societal expectations of relationships. In a world that often places undue pressure on individuals to conform to traditional relationship norms, choosing celibacy can be a powerful act of resistance. It challenges the notion that one must be in a romantic relationship to be happy and fulfilled, and instead encourages individuals to find happiness within themselves.

Moreover, celibacy can be utilized as a means to cultivate a deeper connection with oneself. By embracing solitude and celibacy, individuals can embark on a journey of self-discovery and self-acceptance. This inward focus allows for a more profound understanding of one's desires, values, and purpose in life.

Additionally, celibacy provides a unique opportunity to explore alternative forms of intimacy and relationships. By freeing oneself from the constraints of physical intimacy, individuals can explore and develop deep connections with others based on emotional, intellectual, and spiritual bonds. This alternative approach to relationships can be incredibly fulfilling and transformative.

Celibacy also challenges traditional gender roles and expectations. By choosing celibacy, individuals can reject the notion that one's worth or identity is tied to their ability to form romantic or sexual relationships.

This rejection of traditional gender roles empowers individuals to define their own identities and live authentically.

Lastly, celibacy serves as a means of preserving personal energy and vitality. By abstaining from sexual relationships, individuals can redirect their energy towards personal goals, creative pursuits, and physical well-being. This preservation of energy allows for increased focus, vitality, and overall life satisfaction.

In conclusion, the concept of celibacy in religion offers Catholics a myriad of opportunities for spiritual enlightenment, personal growth, self-discipline, activism, career focus, mental and emotional well-being, rebellion against societal expectations, deeper self-connection, exploration of alternative relationships, challenging traditional gender roles, and preserving personal energy and vitality. By embracing celibacy, individuals can embark on a transformative journey of self-discovery, inner peace, and personal fulfillment.

Historical Perspectives on Celibacy in Catholicism

Throughout the history of Catholicism, celibacy has played a significant role in the lives of clergy members and religious communities. This subchapter aims to explore the historical perspectives on celibacy within the Catholic Church, shedding light on its evolution and significance for Catholics today.

Celibacy for spiritual enlightenment has been a long-standing tradition within Catholicism. The early Church Fathers viewed celibacy as a means to deepen one's commitment to God and fully devote oneself to the service of the Church. By abstaining from sexual relations, individuals could focus their energy on spiritual growth and attaining a closer union with the divine.

Celibacy for personal growth and self-discipline has also been emphasized throughout Catholic history. By renouncing physical desires, individuals were challenged to develop self-control, discipline, and mastery over their bodies. This practice aimed to foster personal growth and strengthen one's character, enabling individuals to become more virtuous and spiritually mature.

Moreover, celibacy has been seen as a form of activism against societal pressures. By choosing celibacy, individuals challenge the prevailing cultural norms that often prioritize physical pleasure and instant gratification. By embracing celibacy, Catholics can live counter-culturally and exemplify alternative ways of finding fulfillment and meaning in life.

Celibacy has also been considered a means to focus on career or personal goals. By abstaining from romantic relationships and family life, individuals can dedicate their time and energy entirely to their chosen vocations. This allows them to pursue their ambitions, excel in their chosen fields, and make a significant impact in their respective spheres.

Additionally, celibacy has been embraced as a way to prioritize mental and emotional well-being. By removing the complexities and potential challenges of intimate relationships, individuals can focus on developing their inner selves, cultivating emotional stability, and nurturing their mental health.

For some, celibacy becomes a form of rebellion against societal expectations of relationships. In a world that often places undue pressure on finding a romantic partner or conforming to traditional relationship expectations, celibacy becomes a radical choice to assert one's independence and challenge societal norms.

Celibacy can also serve as a means to cultivate a deeper connection with oneself. By abstaining from sexual relationships, individuals can redirect their energy inward, exploring their own desires, dreams, and aspirations.

This introspective journey allows for self-discovery and the development of a strong sense of self.

Furthermore, celibacy provides a unique opportunity to explore alternative forms of intimacy and relationships. By abstaining from sexual relations, individuals can explore and cultivate deep connections with others through friendship, mentorship, and spiritual companionship. These alternative forms of intimacy can be equally fulfilling and meaningful.

Moreover, choosing celibacy challenges traditional gender roles and expectations. By embracing celibacy, individuals break free from societal expectations that often place men and women in predetermined roles within relationships. This choice allows for the formation of new paradigms of equality and empowerment.

Lastly, celibacy can serve as a means of preserving personal energy and vitality. By abstaining from sexual activities, individuals can harness and redirect their sexual energy towards other endeavors, such as creative pursuits, intellectual growth, or spiritual practices. This preservation of energy enhances one's overall vitality and sense of purpose.

In conclusion, the historical perspectives on celibacy in Catholicism demonstrate its multifaceted significance for individuals seeking spiritual enlightenment, personal growth, self-discipline, activism, career focus, mental and emotional well-being, rebellion, self-connection, alternative relationships, challenging gender roles, and energy preservation. Understanding the historical context of celibacy within the Catholic Church can provide valuable insights for Catholics navigating these various niches of celibacy in their own lives.

The Spiritual Significance of Celibacy in Catholicism

Celibacy has long held a significant role within Catholicism, serving as a symbol of devotion and spiritual enlightenment. In this subchapter, we will explore the spiritual significance of celibacy and its various applications in the lives of Catholics.

For many Catholics, celibacy is seen as a powerful tool for spiritual growth and self-discipline. By abstaining from sexual relationships, individuals can redirect their energy and focus toward their spiritual journey. Celibacy allows Catholics to detach themselves from the distractions and temptations of worldly desires, enabling them to deepen their connection with God and seek spiritual enlightenment.

Moreover, celibacy can be seen as a form of activism against societal pressures. In a world that often places an overemphasis on romantic relationships and sexual intimacy, choosing celibacy challenges these expectations and allows individuals to live their lives in accordance with their own values and beliefs. It is a way to resist the societal pressure to conform and instead prioritize one's own spiritual well-being.

Celibacy can also serve as a means to focus on career or personal goals. By abstaining from romantic relationships, individuals can channel their energy and attention toward their professional aspirations or personal endeavors. This intentional redirection of energy allows for increased productivity and dedication to one's chosen path.

Furthermore, celibacy can be a powerful tool for mental and emotional well-being. It provides an opportunity for individuals to prioritize their own mental health and emotional stability, free from the potential emotional rollercoaster that can accompany romantic relationships. By cultivating a deep connection with oneself, celibacy allows individuals to explore their own needs, desires, and emotions.

In addition, celibacy can challenge traditional gender roles and expectations. By rejecting the idea that one's worth is tied to a romantic partner or sexual relationships, individuals can break free from societal constraints and redefine their own identities. It offers a means to challenge and dismantle the rigid expectations placed upon individuals based on their gender.

Lastly, celibacy serves as a means of preserving personal energy and vitality. By abstaining from sexual activities, individuals can redirect their life force, or prana, toward other aspects of their lives. This preservation of energy allows for increased vitality, focus, and overall well-being.

In conclusion, celibacy holds a profound spiritual significance within Catholicism. It serves as a powerful tool for personal growth, self-discipline, and spiritual enlightenment. From challenging societal expectations to prioritizing mental and emotional well-being, celibacy offers a path to deeper self-connection and exploration. By embracing celibacy, Catholics can cultivate a more profound relationship with themselves and with God.

Chapter 2: Celibacy for Personal Growth and Self-Discipline

Exploring the Benefits of Celibacy for Personal Growth

In today's fast-paced and hyper-connected world, the concept of celibacy may seem outdated or even misunderstood by many. However, for those seeking personal growth, self-discipline, and spiritual enlightenment, celibacy can offer a unique path towards achieving these goals. This subchapter aims to delve into the various benefits that celibacy can provide, specifically addressing the Catholic audience and those interested in the niches of celibacy for personal growth and self-discipline, spiritual enlightenment, and challenging societal expectations.

First and foremost, celibacy allows individuals to focus their energy and attention on their personal goals and career aspirations. By abstaining from intimate relationships, individuals have more time and mental space to dedicate to their passions and ambitions. This heightened focus can lead to increased productivity, creativity, and ultimately, success in various aspects of life.

Moreover, celibacy serves as a powerful tool for prioritizing mental and emotional well-being. By choosing to remain celibate, individuals can free themselves from the emotional rollercoaster that often accompanies romantic relationships. This freedom allows for a deeper connection with oneself, fostering self-awareness, self-love, and inner peace. By prioritizing emotional well-being, individuals can cultivate a healthier relationship with themselves and others.

Celibacy also provides a unique opportunity to challenge societal expectations and rebel against the pressures of conforming to traditional relationship norms. By actively choosing celibacy, individuals can break free from the societal expectations of being in a romantic partnership and instead focus on their own personal growth and fulfillment. This act of rebellion empowers individuals to live life on their own terms and redefine the meaning of happiness and fulfillment.

Furthermore, celibacy can serve as a means of exploring alternative forms of intimacy and relationships. By abstaining from physical intimacy, individuals are encouraged to seek and cultivate deeper connections with others on an emotional, intellectual, and spiritual level. This exploration can lead to profound connections and a greater understanding of oneself and others.

Lastly, celibacy allows individuals to preserve their personal energy and vitality. By abstaining from sexual activity, individuals can redirect their energy towards other areas of life, such as personal growth, creativity, or spiritual practices. This preservation of energy can lead to increased vitality, a heightened sense of purpose, and an overall improved quality of life.

In conclusion, embracing celibacy for personal growth and spiritual enlightenment can be a transformative journey for individuals seeking to challenge societal expectations, cultivate a deeper connection with themselves, and prioritize their mental and emotional well-being. By choosing celibacy, individuals can unlock a world of opportunities for personal growth, self-discovery, and inner peace.

Developing Self-Discipline through Celibacy

In our modern society, where instant gratification and indulgence seem to be the norm, developing self-discipline has become increasingly challenging. However, for those seeking spiritual enlightenment, personal growth, and self-discipline, celibacy can be a powerful tool. This subchapter explores how embracing celibacy can lead to the cultivation of self-discipline, benefiting individuals from various walks of life, including Catholics.

Celibacy for spiritual enlightenment provides individuals with the opportunity to detach themselves from worldly distractions and focus on their inner selves. By abstaining from intimate relationships and sexual desires, individuals can redirect their energy towards spiritual practices and self-reflection. This intentional self-discipline allows them to deepen their connection with a higher power and experience profound spiritual growth.

For those seeking personal growth and self-discipline, celibacy offers a unique path. By abstaining from physical intimacy, individuals can redirect their energy towards personal goals and aspirations. Freed from the distractions of romantic relationships, they can fully commit themselves to their careers, education, or personal projects. This focused dedication helps individuals develop self-discipline, perseverance, and a strong work ethic, leading to personal growth and success.

Celibacy can also be viewed as a form of activism against societal pressures. In a world that often defines personal worth by one's relationship status, celibacy challenges these societal expectations. By choosing celibacy, individuals assert their independence and prioritize their own well-being over conforming to societal norms. This act of rebellion can inspire others to question traditional gender roles, expectations, and societal pressures surrounding relationships.

Furthermore, celibacy can be a means to prioritize mental and emotional well-being. By abstaining from intimate relationships, individuals can focus on healing past wounds, developing self-love, and nurturing their mental and emotional health. This intentional practice allows individuals to cultivate a deeper connection with themselves, fostering self-awareness, self-acceptance, and emotional resilience.

Celibacy also opens the doors to exploring alternative forms of intimacy and relationships. By relinquishing physical intimacy, individuals can discover new ways of connecting with others, such as through deep friendships, emotional intimacy, and spiritual connections. This exploration challenges traditional notions of intimacy and relationships, paving the way for more authentic and fulfilling connections.

Finally, celibacy preserves personal energy and vitality. By abstaining from sexual activities, individuals can harness their sexual energy, redirecting it towards creative endeavors, spiritual practices, and personal growth. This preservation of energy enhances vitality, rejuvenates the mind and body, and promotes overall well-being.

In conclusion, celibacy offers Catholics and individuals exploring celibacy for personal growth, self-discipline, or spiritual enlightenment a unique opportunity to develop self-discipline. By embracing celibacy, individuals can detach themselves from worldly distractions, prioritize personal goals, challenge societal expectations, cultivate a deeper connection with oneself, explore alternative forms of intimacy, challenge traditional gender roles, and preserve personal energy and vitality. Through self-discipline, individuals can embark on a transformative journey towards spiritual enlightenment, personal growth, and a more fulfilling life.

Nurturing Spiritual Growth through Celibacy

In the realm of spirituality, the concept of celibacy has long been regarded as a powerful means of achieving spiritual growth and enlightenment. Celibacy, the conscious decision to abstain from sexual relationships, is often seen as a noble path that allows individuals to transcend their own human nature and embrace a deeper connection with the divine. This subchapter explores the profound impact of celibacy on spiritual development, particularly within the context of the Catholic faith.

To be celibate is to fight against your own human nature – a struggle that is deeply intertwined with the pursuit of spiritual enlightenment. In Catholicism, celibacy is not only a personal commitment but also a sacred vow taken by clergy members. By embracing this path, these individuals dedicate their lives entirely to serving God and their communities, forsaking personal relationships and desires.

Celibacy is not an easy journey. It requires great discipline, self-control, and a strong conviction in one's spiritual calling. However, it is precisely through this struggle that individuals can nurture their spiritual growth. By consciously denying the physical desires and focusing on the spiritual realm, celibacy becomes a powerful tool for self-transformation.

In the absence of sexual relationships, individuals are encouraged to redirect their energy towards spiritual practices such as prayer, meditation, and contemplation. This redirection allows for a heightened sense of awareness and a deeper connection with the divine. Through celibacy, Catholics can cultivate a profound intimacy with God, experiencing a spiritual union that surpasses the physical realm.

Moreover, celibacy offers individuals the opportunity to cultivate virtues such as chastity, humility, and selflessness. By abstaining from sexual desires, one can learn to overcome the ego and embrace a life centered on love and service. This selflessness is not only directed towards God but also towards the community, as celibate individuals are often called to serve others in various capacities.

While celibacy may seem challenging and contrary to our human nature, it is precisely through this struggle that spiritual growth becomes possible. The commitment to celibacy allows Catholics to transcend their own limitations, surrendering to a higher purpose and embracing a deeper connection with the divine. By nurturing their spiritual growth through celibacy, individuals can experience profound enlightenment, finding solace and purpose in their sacred solitude.

Chapter 3: Celibacy as a Form of Activism Against Societal Pressures

Challenging Cultural Norms and Expectations

In today's society, it is often difficult to break free from cultural norms and expectations. However, embracing celibacy can be a powerful way to challenge these societal pressures and find personal growth, self-discipline, and spiritual enlightenment. This subchapter in "Sacred Solitude: Embracing Celibacy for Spiritual Enlightenment" aims to address the Catholic audience and various niches that celibacy can cater to, including those seeking personal growth, rebellion against societal expectations, career or personal goals, mental and emotional well-being, and alternative forms of intimacy and relationships.

For Catholics, celibacy has traditionally been associated with religious vocations such as priesthood or religious life. However, it is important to recognize that celibacy can also be a personal choice that brings about spiritual enlightenment. By abstaining from sexual relationships, individuals can redirect their energy towards their spiritual journey and deepen their connection with themselves and their faith. This intentional solitude allows Catholics to find solace in their relationship with God and discover a sacredness within themselves.

Moreover, celibacy can serve as a form of activism against societal pressures. In a culture that often measures success and happiness by one's relationship status, choosing celibacy challenges these expectations and redefines the meaning of fulfillment. By consciously opting out of conventional relationships, individuals can prioritize their mental and emotional well-being, focusing on their personal goals and career aspirations. In doing so, they resist the pressure to conform and create a space for personal growth and self-discipline.

Celibacy also provides a platform for individuals to challenge traditional gender roles and expectations. By rejecting societal norms that dictate one's worth based on their relationship status, individuals can break free from the constraints of gender stereotypes and redefine their own sense of identity. This rebellion against societal expectations empowers individuals to live authentically and cultivate a sense of personal freedom.

Furthermore, celibacy offers a unique opportunity to explore alternative forms of intimacy and relationships. By abstaining from sexual encounters, individuals can discover new ways of connecting with others on a deeper emotional and intellectual level. This opens the door to cultivate meaningful friendships and explore the richness of non-sexual connections.

Lastly, celibacy allows individuals to preserve their personal energy and vitality. By abstaining from sexual activities, individuals can redirect their life force towards their personal growth, creativity, and overall well-being. This practice enables them to maintain a high level of energy and focus on their goals and aspirations.

In conclusion, challenging cultural norms and expectations through embracing celibacy can bring about spiritual enlightenment, personal growth, self-discipline, and activism against societal pressures. By prioritizing mental and emotional well-being, exploring alternative forms of intimacy, and challenging traditional gender roles, individuals can cultivate a deeper connection with themselves and live authentically. Ultimately, celibacy serves as a powerful tool for preserving personal energy and vitality, allowing individuals to thrive in all aspects of their lives.

Embracing a Countercultural Lifestyle through Celibacy

In today's hyper-sexualized and relationship-focused society, embracing celibacy may seem like a countercultural choice. However, for those seeking spiritual enlightenment, personal growth, self-discipline, or a means of challenging societal pressures, celibacy can be a powerful and transformative path.

For Catholics, the choice to embrace celibacy is deeply rooted in their faith. It is seen as a way to commit oneself fully to God, to live a life of purity and devotion. By choosing celibacy, Catholics can detach themselves from worldly desires and distractions, allowing them to focus their energy on their spiritual journey.

But celibacy goes beyond religious devotion. It is also a means of personal growth and self-discipline. By abstaining from sexual relationships, individuals can redirect their energy and focus towards their personal goals and aspirations. Celibacy becomes a way to prioritize one's career, education, or personal development. It offers the opportunity to delve deeper into oneself, to discover hidden talents and passions, and to cultivate a greater sense of self-awareness.

In a society that often pressures individuals into conforming to traditional relationship expectations, celibacy can be seen as an act of activism. It challenges societal norms and expectations, refusing to adhere to the idea that a romantic relationship is the ultimate source of happiness and fulfillment. By embracing celibacy, individuals can inspire others to question societal pressures and find alternative paths to fulfillment.

Moreover, celibacy is a powerful tool for prioritizing mental and emotional well-being. It allows individuals to focus on their own needs, to heal from past wounds, and to nurture their mental and emotional health. By choosing celibacy, individuals can break free from toxic relationship patterns, avoid emotional dependencies, and cultivate a deeper connection with themselves.

Furthermore, celibacy offers the opportunity to explore alternative forms of intimacy and relationships. It challenges the notion that physical intimacy is the only way to connect with others. By abstaining from sexual relationships, individuals can develop deeper emotional connections, practice non-sexual forms of intimacy, and explore the richness of platonic relationships.

Celibacy also challenges traditional gender roles and expectations. It allows individuals to break free from societal pressures to conform to specific relationship dynamics. By choosing celibacy, individuals can challenge the notion that their worth and identity are tied to their relationship status, allowing them to redefine their own sense of self and purpose.

Lastly, celibacy serves as a means of preserving personal energy and vitality. By abstaining from sexual relationships, individuals can redirect their life force energy towards personal growth, creativity, and spiritual practices. This preservation of energy can contribute to a greater sense of vitality, clarity, and overall well-being.

In conclusion, embracing celibacy can be a powerful and countercultural choice. Whether motivated by spiritual enlightenment, personal growth, self-discipline, activism, career aspirations, mental and emotional well-being, rebellion against societal expectations, or alternative forms of intimacy, celibacy offers a transformative path for Catholics seeking a deeper connection with themselves and the world around them.

Resisting Consumerism and Materialism through Celibacy

In today's consumer-driven world, where material possessions and instant gratification often take center stage, embracing celibacy can serve as a powerful tool for resisting consumerism and materialism. By choosing to live a life free from sexual relationships, individuals can redirect their focus towards cultivating spiritual enlightenment, personal growth, self-discipline, and challenging societal pressures.

For Catholics seeking a deeper connection with their faith, celibacy can be a transformative path towards spiritual enlightenment. By abstaining from sexual relationships, individuals can devote more time and energy to prayer, meditation, and exploring their relationship with the divine. Through this intentional practice, they may experience a heightened sense of spiritual connection and a deeper understanding of their purpose in life.

Celibacy also offers a unique opportunity for personal growth and self-discipline. By abstaining from sexual relationships, individuals can redirect their energy towards personal development and achieving their goals. Whether it be pursuing a career, academic achievements, or personal passions, celibacy allows for undivided attention and unwavering focus. It offers a chance to prioritize personal goals and aspirations without the distractions that often come with romantic relationships.

Furthermore, celibacy can be seen as a form of activism against societal pressures. By rejecting the notion that happiness and fulfillment can only be found through consumerism and material possessions, individuals who choose celibacy challenge the status quo. They demonstrate that meaningful connections and personal fulfillment can be achieved through self-reflection, self-care, and cultivating deep relationships with oneself and others.

Celibacy also provides an opportunity to focus on mental and emotional well-being. By removing the pressures and expectations that often come with romantic relationships, individuals can prioritize their mental and emotional health. They can focus on self-care, healing, and personal growth, allowing them to cultivate a strong sense of self and emotional resilience.

Moreover, celibacy can be viewed as a form of rebellion against societal expectations of relationships. In a world that often emphasizes the importance of romantic partnerships, celibacy challenges these expectations and encourages individuals to live life on their own terms. It offers a chance to break free from societal norms and explore alternative forms of intimacy and relationships, allowing for personal growth and self-discovery.

Additionally, celibacy can challenge traditional gender roles and expectations. By embracing celibacy, individuals can assert their independence and reject the notion that their worth is tied to their relationship status. It allows them to redefine their identity outside of societal expectations, empowering them to challenge gender roles and pave the way for greater equality and freedom of choice.

Lastly, celibacy serves as a means of preserving personal energy and vitality. By abstaining from sexual relationships, individuals can redirect their energy towards personal pursuits, creativity, and overall well-being. It offers a chance to harness and channel one's energy in a way that promotes vitality and personal fulfillment.

In conclusion, embracing celibacy can be a powerful tool for resisting consumerism and materialism in today's society. For Catholics seeking spiritual enlightenment, personal growth, self-discipline, and a means of activism against societal pressures, celibacy offers a path towards a more meaningful and fulfilling life. It allows individuals to prioritize their mental and emotional well-being, challenge traditional gender roles, and cultivate a deeper connection with oneself. Ultimately, celibacy is a means of preserving personal energy and vitality, enabling individuals to live life on their own terms and resist the pressures of consumerism and materialism.

Chapter 4: Celibacy as a Means to Focus on Career or Personal Goals

Prioritizing Professional Success through Celibacy

In today's fast-paced world, achieving professional success is often seen as a top priority for individuals in various walks of life. However, amidst the hustle and bustle, many find it challenging to strike a balance between their personal and professional lives. This subchapter explores the profound benefits of celibacy as a powerful tool for prioritizing professional success.

For Catholics seeking spiritual enlightenment, celibacy offers a unique path towards a deeper connection with oneself and the divine. By abstaining from intimate relationships, individuals can channel their energy and focus towards their spiritual growth, allowing them to cultivate a profound sense of inner peace and clarity. This intentional solitude becomes a sacred space for personal reflection, prayer, and meditation, enabling individuals to tap into their true potential and find their purpose in life.

Celibacy is not only a means for spiritual awakening but also a powerful tool for personal growth and self-discipline. By refraining from physical intimacy, individuals can redirect their energy towards personal development, acquiring new skills, and pursuing their career or personal goals. With a clear and focused mind, one can channel their energy towards professional endeavors, ultimately leading to greater success and achievement.

Moreover, embracing celibacy can serve as a form of activism against societal pressures and expectations. It challenges the notion that one's worth and happiness are solely reliant on romantic relationships. By choosing celibacy, individuals break free from the confines of societal expectations and empower themselves to live on their own terms. This rebellion against societal norms not only frees individuals from the pressures of conforming but also empowers them to explore alternative forms of intimacy and relationships that may be more aligned with their true selves.

Celibacy also offers a means to prioritize mental and emotional well-being. In a world where relationships can be emotionally taxing, celibacy provides a respite from the complexities of romantic entanglements. By choosing to remain celibate, individuals can focus on their mental and emotional well-being, nurturing themselves and building a solid foundation of self-love and self-care.

Furthermore, celibacy serves as a means of preserving personal energy and vitality. By abstaining from sexual activity, individuals can harness their life force energy and redirect it towards their professional pursuits. This preservation of energy allows for increased focus, creativity, and productivity, leading to enhanced professional success.

In conclusion, celibacy offers a multitude of benefits for individuals looking to prioritize their professional success. Whether seeking spiritual enlightenment, personal growth, self-discipline, or a means to challenge societal expectations, embracing celibacy can unlock new levels of personal and professional achievement. By choosing to prioritize celibacy, individuals can tap into their true potential and lead a life of purpose and fulfillment.

Cultivating Personal Ambitions and Achievements

In the journey towards spiritual enlightenment, celibacy can serve as a powerful tool for personal growth and self-discipline. By embracing celibacy, Catholics have the opportunity to focus their energy and attention on their individual aspirations and achievements. This subchapter explores the various ways in which celibacy can be utilized as a means to cultivate personal ambitions and attain greater fulfillment.

Celibacy for spiritual enlightenment encourages individuals to prioritize their mental and emotional well-being. By abstaining from intimate relationships, individuals can fully devote themselves to their own personal growth and self-discovery. This intentional solitude allows Catholics to delve deep into their inner selves, nurturing a stronger connection with their spiritual essence.

Moreover, celibacy can act as a form of rebellion against societal expectations of relationships. By choosing to live a celibate life, individuals challenge traditional gender roles and expectations, breaking free from societal pressures. This act of defiance empowers Catholics to forge their own path and define success on their own terms.

Celibacy also provides an opportunity to explore alternative forms of intimacy and relationships. By abstaining from physical intimacy, individuals can redirect their focus towards cultivating meaningful connections based on emotional and intellectual intimacy. This shift in perspective allows for deeper and more fulfilling relationships, not solely dependent on physical attraction.

Furthermore, celibacy can serve as a means to prioritize career or personal goals. By abstaining from intimate relationships, individuals can channel their energy towards professional growth or personal aspirations. This heightened focus and dedication to their ambitions can lead to significant achievements and personal fulfillment.

Additionally, celibacy as a form of activism against societal pressures fosters a sense of rebellion. By consciously choosing celibacy, individuals challenge the notion that relationships are the ultimate measure of happiness and success. This rebellious act can inspire others to question societal norms and expectations, paving the way for a more authentic and fulfilling life.

Lastly, celibacy as a means of preserving personal energy and vitality is a vital aspect of cultivating personal ambitions and achievements. By redirecting their sexual energy towards personal growth and self-improvement, individuals can harness their inner power and vitality. This preserved energy can be channeled into various endeavors, propelling individuals towards their goals and aspirations.

In conclusion, celibacy offers a multitude of benefits for Catholics seeking personal growth, self-discipline, and spiritual enlightenment. By embracing celibacy, individuals can prioritize their mental and emotional well-being, challenge societal expectations, focus on personal goals, cultivate deeper connections with themselves, explore alternative forms of intimacy, challenge traditional gender roles, and preserve personal energy and vitality. By harnessing the power of celibacy, Catholics can cultivate their personal ambitions and achieve a greater sense of fulfillment in life.

Balancing Personal Goals with Relationships through Celibacy

In today's fast-paced and interconnected world, it can be challenging to find a balance between pursuing personal goals and maintaining fulfilling relationships. However, embracing celibacy can offer a unique path towards achieving this delicate equilibrium. In this subchapter, we will explore the various ways in which celibacy can benefit individuals seeking spiritual enlightenment, personal growth, self-discipline, and more.

For Catholics, celibacy is often seen as a sacred practice that allows individuals to devote themselves fully to their faith and spiritual journey. By abstaining from sexual relationships, one can focus their energy and attention on deepening their connection with God and exploring the depths of their spirituality. Celibacy becomes a powerful tool to create a space for divine revelation and personal transformation.

Furthermore, celibacy offers an avenue for personal growth and self-discipline. By refraining from physical intimacy, individuals can redirect their energy towards developing their talents, pursuing education, or honing their skills. Celibacy becomes a means to prioritize personal goals, whether it be advancing in a career, engaging in creative pursuits, or embarking on a journey of self-discovery.

Celibacy can also be viewed as a form of activism against societal pressures. In a world obsessed with instant gratification and materialistic pursuits, choosing celibacy challenges the notion that romantic relationships are the ultimate source of happiness and fulfillment. By embracing celibacy, individuals can defy societal expectations and redefine their relationships with themselves and others.

Moreover, celibacy can be a powerful tool for prioritizing mental and emotional well-being. By abstaining from sexual relationships, individuals can cultivate a deep sense of self-awareness and emotional stability. Celibacy allows for introspection and introspection, providing a space for healing and personal growth that is often neglected in the chaos of romantic relationships.

Beyond personal growth, celibacy can also serve as a form of rebellion against societal expectations of relationships. By choosing celibacy, individuals challenge the traditional gender roles and expectations that often accompany romantic partnerships. It becomes a means to break free from the constraints of societal norms and explore alternative forms of intimacy and relationships.

Lastly, celibacy is a way to preserve personal energy and vitality. By abstaining from sexual relationships, individuals can harness their life force energy and direct it towards their goals and aspirations. Celibacy becomes a powerful tool for maintaining physical, mental, and spiritual well-being.

In conclusion, celibacy offers a unique and transformative path towards achieving a balance between personal goals and relationships. Whether it be for spiritual enlightenment, personal growth, or self-discipline, embracing celibacy allows individuals to prioritize their own well-being and journey towards a deeper connection with themselves and the world around them.

Chapter 5: Celibacy as a Way to Prioritize Mental and Emotional Well-being

Exploring the Connection between Celibacy and Mental Health

In today's fast-paced and demanding world, it can be challenging to find the time and space to prioritize our mental and emotional well-being. However, there is a powerful tool that has been utilized for centuries - celibacy. In this subchapter, we will delve into the fascinating and often overlooked connection between celibacy and mental health.

For Catholics seeking celibacy as a means to achieve spiritual enlightenment, it is crucial to understand the profound impact it can have on mental well-being. By abstaining from sexual relationships and redirecting that energy towards spiritual practices like prayer and meditation, individuals can experience enhanced focus, clarity, and a deeper connection with oneself. This form of self-discipline can lead to personal growth and a profound sense of inner peace.

Moreover, choosing celibacy as a form of activism against societal pressures can have a transformative impact on mental health. In a world that places immense importance on relationships and romantic partnerships, celibacy challenges traditional gender roles and expectations. By rebelling against societal expectations, individuals can break free from the constraints of societal norms and forge their own path. This liberation can contribute to reduced stress, increased self-esteem, and improved mental well-being.

Celibacy can also serve as a tool to prioritize mental and emotional well-being. By abstaining from sexual relationships, individuals can focus their energy and attention on self-care and personal goals. This intentional focus allows for the cultivation of a deeper connection with oneself, leading to increased self-awareness and a heightened sense of purpose.

Furthermore, celibacy offers a unique opportunity to explore alternative forms of intimacy and relationships, challenging the notion that physical intimacy is the only path to fulfillment. By redirecting energy towards cultivating deep emotional connections, individuals can discover new and profound ways of experiencing intimacy, fostering mental well-being and personal growth.

Lastly, celibacy can be a means of preserving personal energy and vitality. By abstaining from sexual relationships, individuals can redirect their life force energy towards personal endeavors, such as career goals or creative pursuits. This preservation of energy can lead to increased focus, productivity, and a heightened sense of vitality, positively impacting mental and emotional well-being.

In conclusion, celibacy, when embraced consciously and intentionally, can have a profound impact on mental health. By exploring the connection between celibacy and mental well-being, Catholics can harness the transformative power of celibacy for spiritual enlightenment, personal growth, self-discipline, activism, and the preservation of personal energy. Embracing celibacy as a tool for mental and emotional well-being allows individuals to prioritize their own needs, challenge societal expectations, and cultivate a deeper connection with oneself.

Nurturing Emotional Well-being through Celibacy

Celibacy, often associated with religious devotion, has long been perceived as a means to achieve spiritual enlightenment. However, its benefits extend beyond the realm of spirituality and can significantly contribute to personal growth, self-discipline, mental and emotional well-being, and even activism against societal pressures. In this subchapter, we will explore how embracing celibacy can positively impact various aspects of our lives.

For Catholics seeking spiritual enlightenment, celibacy can be a powerful tool. By abstaining from sexual relationships, individuals can redirect their focus and energy towards their spiritual journey. Celibacy allows for a deeper connection with oneself and the divine, fostering a sense of inner peace and tranquility. It creates a sacred space for introspection and meditation, enabling individuals to explore their spirituality on a profound level.

Moreover, celibacy can also serve as a means to prioritize mental and emotional well-being. In a world that often prioritizes romantic relationships, celibacy offers a unique opportunity to center oneself and cultivate a healthy relationship with one's emotions. By abstaining from intimate relationships, individuals can focus on self-care, self-reflection, and personal growth. This intentional period of solitude allows for the development of emotional intelligence, self-awareness, and resilience.

Celibacy can also be viewed as a form of activism against societal pressures. In a world that constantly bombards us with unrealistic expectations of relationships and sexuality, choosing celibacy is an act of rebellion. It challenges the notion that our worth is determined by our romantic partnerships. By embracing celibacy, individuals can take a stand against societal norms and redefine their own path to happiness and fulfillment.

Furthermore, celibacy can be a valuable tool for individuals looking to focus on their career or personal goals. By eliminating the distractions of romantic relationships, individuals can channel their energy and dedication towards their ambitions. It provides a platform for professional growth and self-fulfillment, allowing individuals to achieve their full potential.

Lastly, celibacy preserves personal energy and vitality. By abstaining from sexual relationships, individuals can redirect their sexual energy towards creative pursuits, physical well-being, and personal development. It allows for the cultivation of a more profound connection with oneself and others, unburdened by societal expectations and traditional gender roles.

In conclusion, celibacy offers numerous benefits for Catholics seeking spiritual enlightenment, personal growth, self-discipline, and emotional well-being. It provides a means to challenge societal pressures, prioritize personal goals, and cultivate a deeper connection with oneself. By embracing celibacy, individuals can embark on a transformative journey of self-discovery and empowerment.

Self-Care and Self-Reflection in Celibacy

Self-care and self-reflection are essential components of living a fulfilling and enlightened life in the context of celibacy. In this subchapter, we will explore how celibacy can provide a unique opportunity for Catholics to prioritize their mental, emotional, and physical well-being while also challenging societal expectations and norms.

Celibacy for spiritual enlightenment is a path that requires individuals to embark on a journey of self-discovery and introspection. By abstaining from intimate relationships, one can redirect their energy inward and focus on cultivating a deeper connection with themselves. This intentional solitude allows for the exploration of personal beliefs, values, and spirituality, leading to spiritual growth and enlightenment.

Moreover, celibacy provides an avenue for personal growth and self-discipline. By choosing to abstain from sexual relationships, individuals are forced to confront their desires and impulses, leading to a heightened level of self-awareness and self-control. This self-discipline can then be extended to other aspects of life, such as career goals, personal ambitions, and the pursuit of excellence.

Celibacy can also be viewed as a form of activism against societal pressures. In a world that often places a high value on relationships and sexual intimacy, choosing celibacy challenges these societal norms and expectations. By embracing celibacy, individuals can defy the notion that one's worth is solely defined by their relationship status, and instead focus on personal growth, fulfillment, and the pursuit of their passions.

Additionally, celibacy allows individuals to prioritize their mental and emotional well-being. By removing the distractions and potential emotional turmoil that can come with romantic relationships, one can create space for self-reflection, self-care, and emotional healing. This intentional focus on mental and emotional health can lead to greater self-awareness, self-acceptance, and overall happiness.

Furthermore, celibacy can be seen as a rebellion against societal expectations of relationships. By choosing to live a celibate life, individuals challenge traditional gender roles and expectations, freeing themselves from the pressures of conforming to societal norms. This rebellion allows for the exploration of alternative forms of intimacy and relationships, fostering a greater sense of freedom and authenticity.

Lastly, celibacy serves as a means of preserving personal energy and vitality. By abstaining from sexual activity, individuals can redirect their energy towards personal pursuits, creativity, and self-care. This preservation of energy allows for increased focus, productivity, and a heightened sense of vitality in all aspects of life.

In conclusion, self-care and self-reflection are crucial aspects of celibacy for spiritual enlightenment. By embracing celibacy, individuals can prioritize their mental, emotional, and physical well-being while challenging societal expectations, cultivating a deeper connection with oneself, and exploring alternative forms of intimacy and relationships. Celibacy serves as a tool for personal growth, rebellion against societal pressures, and preservation of personal energy and vitality.

Chapter 6: Celibacy as a Form of Rebellion Against Societal Expectations of Relationships

Rejecting Societal Pressure to be in a Relationship

In a world where being in a relationship is often considered the norm, it can be challenging to resist the societal pressure to conform. However, embracing celibacy for spiritual enlightenment can offer a unique path to personal growth, self-discipline, and rebellion against societal expectations. This subchapter explores the various reasons why one might choose celibacy and how it can positively impact different aspects of life.

For Catholics seeking spiritual enlightenment, celibacy serves as a powerful tool. By abstaining from physical intimacy, individuals can redirect their focus inward, allowing them to deepen their connection with the divine. Through sacred solitude, they can explore their spirituality, engage in introspection, and cultivate a more profound understanding of themselves and their place in the world.

Celibacy also provides an opportunity for personal growth and self-discipline. By rejecting the distractions that come with romantic relationships, individuals can channel their energy into pursuing personal goals and career aspirations. This intentional focus allows for self-improvement, skill development, and the realization of one's full potential.

Moreover, celibacy can be seen as a form of activism against societal pressures. By refusing to conform to societal expectations of relationships, individuals challenge the notion that one's worth is dependent on being in a partnership. This act of rebellion empowers others to question traditional gender roles and expectations, paving the way for a more inclusive and accepting society.

Furthermore, celibacy serves as a means to prioritize mental and emotional well-being. In a fast-paced world, taking the time to nurture one's mental and emotional health is crucial. By refraining from romantic relationships, individuals can focus on self-care, engage in therapy, and cultivate a deeper understanding of their own needs, leading to enhanced overall well-being.

Celibacy also provides a unique opportunity to explore alternative forms of intimacy and relationships. By removing the emphasis on physical connection, individuals can build deep, meaningful connections based on emotional, intellectual, and spiritual bonds. This exploration challenges societal norms and opens doors to new possibilities for connection and fulfillment.

Lastly, celibacy serves as a means of preserving personal energy and vitality. By abstaining from physical intimacy, individuals can redirect their life force energy towards personal growth, creativity, and spiritual pursuits. This preservation of energy allows for increased vitality, focus, and a stronger connection with oneself.

In conclusion, rejecting societal pressure to be in a relationship and embracing celibacy can lead to profound personal growth, spiritual enlightenment, and rebellion against societal expectations. By prioritizing one's mental and emotional well-being, career aspirations, and exploration of alternative forms of intimacy, individuals can cultivate a deeper connection with themselves and challenge traditional gender roles. Ultimately, celibacy becomes a powerful tool for preserving personal energy and vitality, allowing individuals to live a life of authenticity and purpose.

Embracing Independence and Freedom through Celibacy

In a society that often equates happiness and fulfillment with romantic relationships, it takes a certain level of courage and self-awareness to embrace celibacy. Celibacy, contrary to popular belief, is not about depriving oneself of physical intimacy or love. Instead, it is a conscious choice to prioritize personal growth, self-discipline, and spiritual enlightenment.

For Catholics seeking to embark on a journey of celibacy, it is essential to understand the profound impact it can have on various aspects of life. Celibacy is not solely about abstaining from sexual relationships; it is a powerful tool that allows individuals to focus on their careers, personal goals, mental and emotional well-being, and even challenge societal expectations.

By choosing celibacy, one can break free from the pressures of societal norms and expectations, particularly in the realm of relationships. In a culture that often places excessive emphasis on finding a partner, celibacy can be seen as an act of rebellion against these expectations. It allows individuals to prioritize their own happiness and well-being above conforming to societal standards.

Moreover, embracing celibacy can lead to a deeper connection with oneself. By abstaining from external distractions and desires, individuals can explore their own thoughts, emotions, and spiritual beliefs. Celibacy allows for introspection and self-discovery, fostering a stronger relationship with one's own identity and purpose.

Additionally, celibacy can open doors to alternative forms of intimacy and relationships. By removing the focus on physicality, individuals can cultivate deeper connections based on emotional, intellectual, and spiritual compatibility. This form of intimacy goes beyond societal expectations and allows for authentic and fulfilling connections.

Celibacy can also challenge traditional gender roles and expectations. In a world where relationships often come with predefined roles and responsibilities, choosing celibacy can be a means of breaking free from these limitations. It allows individuals to define their own paths and challenge societal norms, promoting equality and individual autonomy.

Lastly, celibacy can preserve personal energy and vitality. By abstaining from sexual relationships, individuals can redirect their energy towards personal growth, creativity, and spiritual pursuits. This preservation of energy can lead to increased focus, productivity, and overall well-being.

In conclusion, embracing celibacy can be a transformative journey that fosters independence, freedom, and self-discovery. For Catholics seeking spiritual enlightenment, personal growth, rebellion against societal pressures, or preservation of energy, celibacy offers a unique path towards fulfillment. By choosing celibacy, individuals can prioritize their own well-being, challenge societal expectations, and cultivate a deeper connection with themselves and others.

Redefining Relationship Norms and Expectations

In today's society, the norms and expectations surrounding relationships have become deeply ingrained in our collective consciousness. However, as Catholics seeking spiritual enlightenment and personal growth, it is crucial to challenge these norms and explore alternative paths. One such path that has gained significant attention is celibacy.

Celibacy, traditionally associated with religious vows, has evolved beyond its religious connotations. It has become a powerful tool for self-discipline, personal growth, and rebellion against societal pressures. By embracing celibacy, individuals can prioritize their mental and emotional well-being, focus on their career or personal goals, and preserve their personal energy and vitality.

For those seeking spiritual enlightenment, celibacy offers a unique opportunity to cultivate a deeper connection with oneself. By abstaining from physical intimacy, individuals can redirect their energy towards self-reflection, meditation, and spiritual practices. This intentional solitude allows for a profound exploration of one's innermost thoughts and desires, ultimately leading to a greater understanding of oneself and the divine.

Celibacy also challenges traditional gender roles and expectations, providing a platform for individuals to break free from societal constraints. By rejecting the notion that romantic relationships define one's worth, individuals can assert their autonomy and redefine their identities. This rebellion against societal expectations can serve as a catalyst for personal growth, empowering individuals to embrace their true selves and pursue their passions fearlessly.

Furthermore, celibacy opens up avenues for exploring alternative forms of intimacy and relationships. By removing the emphasis on physical intimacy, individuals are encouraged to seek emotional, intellectual, and spiritual connections with others. This shift in focus allows for deeper and more meaningful relationships, fostering a sense of interconnectedness and community.

In the book "Sacred Solitude: Embracing Celibacy for Spiritual Enlightenment," we delve into the multifaceted benefits of celibacy. Whether you are seeking spiritual enlightenment, personal growth, rebellion against societal pressures, or a means to prioritize your mental and emotional well-being, this book offers guidance and support on your celibate journey.

It is time to redefine relationship norms and expectations, and embrace celibacy as a transformative and empowering choice. Through celibacy, we can embark on a path of self-discovery, challenge societal expectations, and cultivate a deeper connection with ourselves and the world around us. Let us embark on this sacred journey together and embrace the limitless possibilities that celibacy offers.

Chapter 7: Celibacy as a Means to Cultivate a Deeper Connection with Oneself

Exploring Self-Discovery and Self-Reflection through Celibacy

In the subchapter titled "Exploring Self-Discovery and Self-Reflection through Celibacy," we delve into the profound benefits that embracing celibacy can bring to individuals seeking spiritual enlightenment, personal growth, and self-discipline. This chapter is specifically addressed to the Catholic audience, as well as those interested in the various niches related to celibacy.

Celibacy for spiritual enlightenment is a path chosen by many individuals seeking a deeper connection with their faith and the divine. By abstaining from physical intimacy, one can redirect their energy towards spiritual practices, such as prayer, meditation, and contemplation. Through celibacy, Catholics can explore their inner selves and develop a stronger relationship with God, finding solace and guidance in their solitude.

Moreover, celibacy offers a unique opportunity for personal growth and self-discipline. By abstaining from sexual relationships, individuals can focus on their personal goals and aspirations without the distractions that often accompany romantic involvements. This allows for greater self-reflection, self-discovery, and the cultivation of skills and talents that might have otherwise gone unexplored.

Celibacy can also be viewed as a form of activism against societal pressures. In a world that often equates happiness and fulfillment with romantic relationships, choosing celibacy challenges these expectations. By embracing celibacy, individuals can defy societal norms and prioritize their own well-being, mental and emotional health, and personal growth.

Furthermore, celibacy can serve as a means to focus on one's career or personal goals. By abstaining from romantic relationships, individuals can invest more time, energy, and dedication to their professional pursuits. This choice allows for increased productivity, concentration, and the opportunity to reach higher levels of success.

Celibacy is also a powerful tool for cultivating a deeper connection with oneself. By redirecting the energy that would otherwise be invested in romantic relationships, individuals can explore their own desires, passions, and interests. This self-discovery leads to a greater understanding of one's own needs and desires, fostering self-love and acceptance.

Additionally, celibacy provides a unique opportunity to explore alternative forms of intimacy and relationships. By focusing on emotional and spiritual connections with others, individuals can cultivate deep and meaningful connections that transcend physicality. This exploration challenges traditional notions of relationships and allows for a broader understanding of human connection.

Finally, celibacy allows individuals to challenge traditional gender roles and expectations. By choosing to abstain from sexual relationships, individuals can challenge societal norms that often place pressure on individuals to conform to specific gender roles within relationships. This freedom allows for the exploration and expression of one's true self, free from societal expectations.

In conclusion, celibacy serves as a means of preserving personal energy and vitality while embarking on a journey of self-discovery, self-reflection, and personal growth. For Catholics and those interested in various niches related to celibacy, embracing celibacy can lead to spiritual enlightenment, personal growth, and the cultivation of deep and meaningful connections with oneself and others.

Nurturing Self-Love and Self-Acceptance through Celibacy

In the journey towards spiritual enlightenment, personal growth, and self-discipline, celibacy can serve as a powerful tool. For Catholics seeking a deeper connection with themselves and a means to challenge societal expectations, embracing celibacy can be a transformative experience.

Celibacy allows individuals to prioritize their mental and emotional well-being. By abstaining from sexual relationships, one can dedicate time and energy to self-reflection, self-care, and personal goals. It provides an opportunity to focus on career aspirations and pursue personal dreams without the distractions that come with romantic entanglements.

Moreover, celibacy can be seen as a form of rebellion against societal pressures. In a world that often equates relationships with success and fulfillment, choosing celibacy challenges these expectations and allows individuals to define their own path. It empowers Catholics to break free from traditional gender roles and expectations, fostering a sense of independence and self-confidence.

Through celibacy, individuals can cultivate a deeper connection with themselves. By redirecting energy away from external relationships, one can explore alternative forms of intimacy and relationships, such as friendships, mentorships, and spiritual connections. This exploration allows for a greater understanding of one's desires, boundaries, and values, ultimately leading to a more authentic and fulfilling life.

Furthermore, celibacy serves as a means of preserving personal energy and vitality. By refraining from sexual activities, individuals can harness and direct this energy towards personal growth and spiritual enlightenment. This preservation of energy not only enhances physical well-being but also allows for a heightened spiritual experience and a deeper understanding of oneself.

In embracing celibacy, Catholics can find a path to self-love and self-acceptance. By choosing to focus on their own needs and desires, they honor and nurture themselves. Through this intentional practice of self-care, individuals can develop a profound sense of self-worth and build a strong foundation for personal growth and spiritual enlightenment.

In conclusion, celibacy offers a multitude of benefits for Catholics seeking spiritual enlightenment, personal growth, and self-discipline. It provides a means to challenge societal pressures, prioritize mental and emotional well-being, cultivate a deeper connection with oneself, explore alternative forms of intimacy, challenge traditional gender roles, and preserve personal energy and vitality. By nurturing self-love and self-acceptance through celibacy, individuals can embark on a transformative journey of self-discovery, leading to a more fulfilling and enlightened life.

The Journey of Self-Actualization through Celibacy

In today's fast-paced and hyper-connected world, finding inner peace and achieving self-actualization can seem like an elusive goal. However, for many Catholics, celibacy has become a powerful tool on the path to spiritual enlightenment. In this subchapter, we will delve into the transformative journey of self-actualization through celibacy and explore its various facets.

Celibacy for spiritual enlightenment is a path chosen by individuals seeking a deeper connection with the divine. By abstaining from physical intimacy, one can redirect their energy towards developing a profound spiritual relationship. Through prayer, meditation, and contemplation, celibacy allows Catholics to cultivate a heightened sense of awareness and attunement to the divine presence within and around them.

Furthermore, celibacy offers a unique opportunity for personal growth and self-discipline. By consciously choosing to refrain from sexual relationships, individuals can channel their focus and energy towards personal goals, whether it be excelling in their career or pursuing their passions. Celibacy fosters a sense of discipline and self-mastery, enabling individuals to achieve remarkable feats and unlock their full potential.

Celibacy also serves as a form of activism against societal pressures. In a world obsessed with instant gratification and casual relationships, celibacy challenges the status quo and encourages a deeper exploration of oneself. By resisting societal expectations of relationships, individuals reclaim their autonomy and assert their own values and beliefs.

Moreover, celibacy provides a precious opportunity to prioritize mental and emotional well-being. By stepping away from the distractions and complications of romantic relationships, individuals can focus on nurturing their own mental and emotional health. Celibacy becomes a sanctuary for self-care and self-exploration, allowing individuals to heal and grow in profound ways.

In addition, celibacy serves as a powerful means to rebel against societal expectations of relationships. By choosing to be celibate, individuals challenge traditional gender roles and expectations. They break free from the confines of societal norms and embrace their authentic selves, unencumbered by the pressures of conforming to societal expectations.

Celibacy also offers a unique pathway to cultivating a deeper connection with oneself. By abstaining from physical intimacy, individuals can explore alternative forms of intimacy and relationships, such as deep friendships, spiritual connections, and creative pursuits. This enables them to forge a more authentic and fulfilling relationship with themselves, ultimately leading to self-actualization.

Lastly, celibacy serves as a means of preserving personal energy and vitality. By redirecting sexual energy towards personal growth and spiritual pursuits, individuals tap into a wellspring of vitality and creativity. This energy can be harnessed to achieve extraordinary feats and live a life of purpose and fulfillment.

In conclusion, the journey of self-actualization through celibacy is a profound and transformative path for Catholics. It encompasses various niches, from celibacy for spiritual enlightenment and personal growth to rebellion against societal expectations and the preservation of personal energy. By embracing celibacy, individuals can embark on a sacred solitude that leads to spiritual enlightenment and a deeper connection with oneself.

Chapter 8: Celibacy as a Tool for Exploring Alternative Forms of Intimacy and Relationships

Embracing Platonic Relationships and Intimacy

In the journey of embracing celibacy for spiritual enlightenment, it is crucial to recognize the value and power of platonic relationships and intimacy. While celibacy often involves abstaining from romantic or sexual relationships, it does not mean isolating oneself from meaningful connections with others.

For Catholics who have chosen celibacy as a path to spiritual growth and self-discipline, nurturing platonic relationships can provide a sense of companionship, support, and understanding. These relationships offer a unique opportunity to bond with others on a deep emotional and intellectual level, without the complexities and distractions of romantic or sexual involvement.

Moreover, embracing platonic intimacy can be seen as a form of activism against societal pressures. In a culture that heavily emphasizes romantic and sexual relationships as the ultimate source of fulfillment, choosing celibacy challenges these expectations and encourages a broader perspective on human connection and love. By demonstrating that celibacy can be a valid and fulfilling choice, individuals can inspire others to question societal norms and explore alternative paths to happiness and fulfillment.

Celibacy can also allow individuals to focus on their career or personal goals. By consciously choosing to prioritize their own ambitions and passions over romantic or sexual relationships, individuals can fully dedicate their time, energy, and resources to their professional or personal pursuits. This intentional focus can lead to greater achievements and personal growth, ultimately contributing to a sense of fulfillment and self-realization.

Furthermore, celibacy can be a means to prioritize mental and emotional well-being. By abstaining from romantic or sexual relationships, individuals can redirect their energy towards self-care, self-reflection, and personal healing. This intentional solitude allows for a deeper connection with oneself, enabling individuals to explore their emotions, thoughts, and desires without external distractions or influences.

Celibacy can also be a tool for exploring alternative forms of intimacy and relationships. By removing the emphasis on romantic or sexual involvement, individuals can discover new ways of connecting with others, such as through deep friendships, intellectual partnerships, or spiritual companionship. These platonic relationships can provide profound emotional and intellectual nourishment, fostering personal growth and a sense of fulfillment.

Moreover, choosing celibacy challenges traditional gender roles and expectations. In a society where relationships are often defined by gendered roles and expectations, celibacy can disrupt these norms and open up new possibilities for self-expression and freedom. By embracing celibacy, individuals can redefine their identities outside of societal expectations, empowering themselves and others to challenge traditional gender roles and live authentically.

Lastly, celibacy serves as a means of preserving personal energy and vitality. By abstaining from sexual activity, individuals can redirect their life force towards spiritual and creative endeavors, enhancing their energy levels and overall vitality. This preservation of personal energy can contribute to a greater sense of well-being, clarity, and spiritual enlightenment.

In conclusion, embracing platonic relationships and intimacy is a vital aspect of celibacy for spiritual enlightenment. By nurturing deep connections with others, challenging societal pressures, prioritizing personal goals, focusing on mental and emotional well-being, exploring alternative forms of intimacy, challenging gender roles, and preserving personal energy, individuals can fully embrace celibacy as a path to personal growth, self-discovery, and spiritual enlightenment.

Exploring Non-Sexual Forms of Intimacy

In today's fast-paced and hyper-sexualized world, the concept of celibacy often evokes confusion and misunderstanding. However, for Catholics, and those seeking spiritual enlightenment, celibacy can be a powerful tool for personal growth, self-discipline, and a means to challenge societal pressures.

One of the most intriguing aspects of celibacy is its ability to foster non-sexual forms of intimacy. Contrary to popular belief, intimacy is not solely dependent on physical connection. In fact, celibacy offers a unique opportunity to explore and cultivate alternative forms of intimacy and relationships.

When we remove the focus on sexual gratification, we are able to redirect our attention to deeper emotional connections and spiritual bonding. Without the distractions of physical desires, we can invest our energy in cultivating meaningful relationships with ourselves, others, and the Divine.

Celibacy allows us to prioritize mental and emotional well-being, as it enables us to fully focus on our personal goals and aspirations. By abstaining from sexual relationships, we liberate ourselves from the societal expectations and pressures often associated with traditional relationships. This form of rebellion against societal norms empowers us to challenge traditional gender roles and expectations, forging a path of self-discovery and authenticity.

With celibacy as our guiding principle, we are able to preserve our personal energy and vitality. By abstaining from sexual activity, we channel our energy into other aspects of our lives, such as career, personal goals, and activism. This enables us to make a greater impact on society and create positive change.

Furthermore, celibacy provides us with an opportunity to explore and cultivate a deeper connection with ourselves. By embracing solitude and self-reflection, we gain a profound understanding of our own desires, fears, and aspirations. This self-awareness allows us to navigate life with a sense of clarity and purpose.

Ultimately, celibacy for spiritual enlightenment offers a pathway to transcend the limitations of societal expectations and explore the depths of human connection. By embracing non-sexual forms of intimacy, we discover the transformative power of emotional, spiritual, and intellectual bonds. Through this journey, we uncover a profound sense of self, challenge societal norms, and prioritize personal growth and well-being.

In the pages of "Sacred Solitude: Embracing Celibacy for Spiritual Enlightenment," you will embark on a journey of self-discovery, exploring the myriad benefits of celibacy. This book is a powerful resource for Catholics and individuals seeking to cultivate non-sexual forms of intimacy, challenge societal pressures, and prioritize personal growth and well-being.

Expanding the Definition of Relationships through Celibacy

In our society, relationships are often defined solely by romantic or sexual connections. However, there is a growing movement that recognizes the power and potential of celibacy to expand the definition of relationships.

Celibacy, far from being a restriction or a denial of love, is a powerful tool that can lead to spiritual enlightenment, personal growth, self-discipline, and even activism against societal pressures.

For Catholics seeking spiritual enlightenment, celibacy can be a transformative practice. By refraining from sexual relationships, individuals can redirect their energy towards deepening their connection with their faith and their understanding of the divine. This intentional solitude allows for a focused exploration of one's spirituality, leading to a deeper sense of purpose and fulfillment.

Moreover, celibacy can also be a path towards personal growth and self-discipline. By abstaining from sexual relationships, individuals can channel their energies into personal development, pursuing their passions, and achieving their goals. This intentional focus on personal growth allows for the cultivation of self-discipline and the development of a strong sense of self.

Celibacy can also be a form of activism against societal pressures. In a world where relationships are often seen as the ultimate measure of success, choosing celibacy challenges societal expectations and norms. It is a powerful statement against the pressure to conform to societal ideals and can inspire others to question the importance placed on romantic and sexual relationships.

Furthermore, celibacy can be a means to prioritize mental and emotional well-being. By abstaining from sexual relationships, individuals can create space for self-reflection, healing, and self-care. This intentional solitude allows for the exploration and nurturing of one's mental and emotional well-being, leading to greater self-awareness, emotional stability, and overall happiness.

Celibacy can also be a form of rebellion against societal expectations of relationships. By choosing celibacy, individuals challenge traditional gender roles and expectations, freeing themselves from the limitations imposed by societal norms. This rebellion allows for the exploration of alternative forms of intimacy and relationships, fostering a deeper connection with oneself and others on a non-physical level.

Additionally, celibacy can serve as a means of preserving personal energy and vitality. By abstaining from sexual relationships, individuals can conserve and redirect their energy towards other aspects of their lives. This preservation of personal energy allows for increased focus, productivity, and overall vitality.

In conclusion, expanding the definition of relationships through celibacy is a powerful and transformative practice. It can lead to spiritual enlightenment, personal growth, self-discipline, activism, mental and emotional well-being, rebellion against societal expectations, deeper connections, exploration of alternative forms of intimacy, and preservation of personal energy and vitality. By embracing celibacy, Catholics can embark on a journey towards a more fulfilling and holistic understanding of relationships and themselves.

Chapter 9: Celibacy as a Way to Challenge Traditional Gender Roles and Expectations

Breaking Free from Gender Stereotypes through Celibacy

In today's society, gender stereotypes continue to confine individuals within narrow roles and expectations. However, there is a powerful tool that Catholics can utilize to challenge these societal pressures and break free from these limitations: celibacy. Embracing celibacy for spiritual enlightenment offers a unique opportunity to challenge traditional gender roles and expectations, while prioritizing personal growth, mental and emotional well-being, and career or personal goals.

Celibacy, often associated with religious practices, is a conscious choice to abstain from sexual relationships. It allows individuals to redirect their energy towards their spiritual journey, personal development, and self-discipline. By embracing celibacy, Catholics can liberate themselves from the societal pressures of conforming to traditional gender roles, enabling them to explore alternative forms of intimacy and relationships.

One of the most empowering aspects of celibacy is its potential to serve as a form of rebellion against societal expectations of relationships. By choosing celibacy, individuals challenge the notion that one must be in a romantic relationship to find fulfillment or happiness. This form of activism can inspire others to question societal norms and expectations, ultimately leading to a more inclusive and accepting society.

Moreover, celibacy provides Catholics with an opportunity to prioritize their mental and emotional well-being. It allows individuals to cultivate a deeper connection with oneself, fostering self-awareness, self-love, and self-acceptance. By focusing on personal growth, celibacy becomes a powerful tool for individuals to strengthen their sense of identity and purpose.

Celibacy also offers a means to preserve personal energy and vitality. By abstaining from sexual relationships, individuals can redirect their energy towards their career or personal goals. This focused energy allows them to excel in their chosen path, unlocking new levels of success and fulfillment.

Furthermore, celibacy challenges traditional gender roles by encouraging individuals to break free from societal expectations. It allows men and women to embrace their true selves, unconstrained by stereotypes. By rejecting the notion that one's worth is tied to their relationship status, celibacy empowers individuals to define their own identity and live authentically.

In conclusion, celibacy for spiritual enlightenment provides a powerful means for Catholics to break free from gender stereotypes and societal pressures. By choosing celibacy, individuals can prioritize personal growth, challenge traditional gender roles, and cultivate a deeper connection with oneself. It offers an opportunity to rebel against societal expectations, focus on career or personal goals, and preserve personal energy and vitality. Embracing celibacy not only enriches one's spiritual journey but also contributes to the creation of a more inclusive and accepting society.

Empowering Women through Celibacy

In today's society, women are often faced with numerous pressures and expectations that can hinder their personal growth and self-fulfillment. However, one powerful tool that can help women break free from societal constraints and achieve spiritual enlightenment is celibacy. Celibacy, often associated with religious vows, can be a transformative practice for women, allowing them to prioritize their mental and emotional well-being, focus on their career or personal goals, and challenge traditional gender roles and expectations.

For many women, celibacy offers a unique opportunity to cultivate a deeper connection with oneself. By abstaining from intimate relationships, women can redirect their energy inward and embark on a journey of self-discovery and self-love. Through this process, they can explore their passions, talents, and desires without the distractions of romantic entanglements. Celibacy becomes a tool for women to reconnect with their true essence, paving the way for personal growth and self-discipline.

Furthermore, celibacy can also serve as a form of rebellion against societal pressures. In a world that often places great importance on romantic relationships and traditional gender roles, choosing celibacy challenges these norms and allows women to live life on their own terms. By rejecting the idea that a woman's worth is solely defined by her relationship status, women can reclaim their power and assert their independence.

Celibacy also provides women with the opportunity to preserve their personal energy and vitality. By abstaining from sexual relationships, women can redirect this energy towards their personal and professional endeavors. This newfound focus can lead to greater success and fulfillment in their careers, as well as the pursuit of personal goals and passions.

Moreover, celibacy can be a powerful form of activism against societal pressures. By consciously choosing celibacy, women can defy societal expectations and pave the way for alternative forms of intimacy and relationships. This challenges the notion that romantic relationships are the only path to happiness and fulfillment, opening up a world of possibilities for women to explore different types of connections and relationships.

In conclusion, celibacy is a transformative practice that empowers women in multiple dimensions of life. Whether it is for spiritual enlightenment, personal growth, self-discipline, or rebellion against societal expectations, celibacy allows women to prioritize their mental and emotional well-being, focus on their career or personal goals, and challenge traditional gender roles. By embracing celibacy, women can cultivate a deeper connection with themselves, explore alternative forms of intimacy and relationships, and preserve their personal energy and vitality. It is a powerful tool that enables women to break free from societal constraints and embrace a life of empowerment and self-fulfillment.

Redefining Masculinity and Femininity in Celibacy

In today's society, the concepts of masculinity and femininity are often tied to one's sexual experiences and relationships. However, in the realm of celibacy, these traditional definitions are challenged and redefined. Celibacy offers a unique opportunity to explore and transcend societal expectations, allowing individuals to redefine what it means to be masculine or feminine.

For Catholics embracing celibacy for spiritual enlightenment, the subchapter on redefining masculinity and femininity is particularly relevant. In the pursuit of spiritual growth, individuals are encouraged to detach from worldly desires, including romantic and sexual relationships. By embracing celibacy, Catholics can challenge the notion that masculinity or femininity is solely defined by sexual prowess or attractiveness.

Celibacy for personal growth and self-discipline also provides a platform to redefine gender roles and expectations. In a world where gender stereotypes often limit individuals' potential, celibacy becomes a tool for breaking free from these constraints. By prioritizing personal goals and focusing on self-improvement, individuals can redefine their masculinity or femininity based on qualities such as resilience, discipline, and inner strength.

Moreover, celibacy can serve as a form of rebellion against societal pressures regarding relationships. In a culture that often prioritizes romantic partnerships and pressures individuals to conform to certain relationship norms, choosing celibacy challenges these expectations. By embracing celibacy, individuals can assert their autonomy and redefine their understanding of masculinity and femininity beyond societal expectations.

Celibacy also offers a means to prioritize mental and emotional well-being. In a world that often equates happiness and fulfillment with romantic relationships, celibacy allows individuals to focus on their inner selves. By cultivating a deeper connection with oneself, individuals can redefine their understanding of masculinity and femininity based on self-awareness, emotional intelligence, and personal growth.

By exploring alternative forms of intimacy and relationships, celibacy challenges traditional gender roles and expectations. It provides an avenue to redefine masculinity and femininity based on qualities such as compassion, empathy, and connection beyond physicality. In this way, individuals can redefine their understanding of what it means to be masculine or feminine, emphasizing emotional intimacy and spiritual connection.

Lastly, celibacy can serve as a means of preserving personal energy and vitality. By abstaining from sexual activity, individuals can redirect their energy towards personal goals and pursuits. This redirection allows individuals to redefine their understanding of masculinity and femininity based on ambition, drive, and a sense of purpose.

In conclusion, celibacy for spiritual enlightenment, personal growth, self-discipline, and various other reasons offers a unique opportunity to redefine masculinity and femininity. By challenging societal expectations, individuals can explore alternative forms of intimacy, prioritize mental and emotional well-being, rebel against traditional gender roles, and cultivate a deeper connection with oneself. Celibacy becomes a tool for embracing personal autonomy and redefining what it truly means to be masculine or feminine in a world that often limits these definitions.

Chapter 10: Celibacy as a Means of Preserving Personal Energy and Vitality

Understanding the Energy Dynamics in Celibacy

In the journey of embracing celibacy for spiritual enlightenment, it is crucial to comprehend the energy dynamics at play. Celibacy, a conscious choice to abstain from sexual relations, has profound effects on our physical, emotional, and spiritual well-being. This subchapter seeks to explore the intricate connection between celibacy and energy, shedding light on its various dimensions and benefits for Catholics who are drawn to the path of celibacy for different reasons.

Celibacy, when approached with intention and discipline, can be a powerful tool for harnessing and preserving personal energy and vitality. By redirecting the sexual energy that would have been expended through physical relations, individuals can tap into a wellspring of transformative energy. This surplus of energy can then be channeled towards personal growth, career aspirations, and self-discipline. By consciously conserving and utilizing this energy, celibates can enhance their focus and drive to achieve their goals.

Moreover, celibacy allows individuals to prioritize their mental and emotional well-being. Without the distractions and complications often associated with romantic relationships, celibates can cultivate a deeper connection with themselves. They can engage in self-reflection, introspection, and self-care practices that nourish their inner world. This heightened self-awareness enables them to develop a stronger sense of identity and purpose, leading to personal growth and self-fulfillment.

In addition, celibacy can serve as a form of activism against societal pressures and expectations surrounding relationships. By choosing celibacy, individuals challenge traditional gender roles and expectations, asserting their autonomy and breaking free from societal norms. This act of rebellion empowers them to redefine their own path and live according to their own values, rather than conforming to external pressures.

Furthermore, celibacy opens doors to explore alternative forms of intimacy and relationships. By redirecting their focus from physical intimacy, individuals can cultivate deeper emotional connections, spiritual bonds, and intellectual stimulation with others. This allows them to explore the vast spectrum of human connection beyond the confines of traditional romantic relationships.

Ultimately, understanding the energy dynamics in celibacy is crucial for Catholics who choose this path for various reasons. By embracing celibacy, individuals can harness their energy, prioritize their well-being, challenge societal expectations, and explore alternative forms of intimacy. This subchapter aims to inspire and guide readers in their journey towards spiritual enlightenment through celibacy, empowering them to lead fulfilling and purposeful lives.

Harnessing Sexual Energy for Personal Growth

Celibacy is often associated with religious practices, particularly within the Catholic community. However, it is not merely a practice limited to religion; it can also be a powerful tool for personal growth and self-discipline. In this subchapter, we will explore the concept of harnessing sexual energy for personal growth and how it can benefit individuals in various aspects of their lives.

For those seeking spiritual enlightenment, celibacy can be a transformative practice. By abstaining from sexual activity, individuals can redirect their energy towards spiritual pursuits, allowing them to deepen their connection with the divine. Through meditation, prayer, and introspection, they can cultivate a sense of inner peace and clarity, ultimately leading to spiritual growth.

Celibacy also offers a unique opportunity for individuals to focus on their career or personal goals. By refraining from intimate relationships, one can prioritize their professional aspirations without the distractions that often come with romantic involvement. This allows individuals to channel their energy and efforts into achieving their ambitions, leading to greater success and personal fulfillment.

Moreover, celibacy serves as a means to prioritize mental and emotional well-being. In a society that often places immense pressure on relationships and romantic partnerships, celibacy offers a respite from societal expectations. It allows individuals to focus on self-care, self-love, and emotional healing, fostering a healthier and more balanced state of mind.

Celibacy can also be viewed as a form of rebellion against societal expectations of relationships. It challenges the conventional notion that romantic partnerships are essential for happiness and fulfillment. By choosing celibacy, individuals defy societal norms and assert their independence, embracing their own unique path to personal growth and self-discovery.

Furthermore, celibacy can be a tool for exploring alternative forms of intimacy and relationships. It encourages individuals to cultivate deep connections with themselves and others, beyond the confines of physical intimacy. This opens the door to exploring emotional, intellectual, and spiritual connections, fostering profound and meaningful relationships.

Lastly, celibacy allows individuals to preserve their personal energy and vitality. By abstaining from sexual activity, individuals can harness their sexual energy and redirect it towards other areas of their lives. This energy can be channeled into creative pursuits, physical fitness, and overall well-being, leading to increased vitality and a sense of empowerment.

In conclusion, celibacy has the potential to serve as a catalyst for personal growth and self-discovery. Whether it is practiced for spiritual enlightenment, self-discipline, or challenging societal expectations, celibacy offers individuals the opportunity to harness their sexual energy and redirect it towards various aspects of their lives. By embracing celibacy, individuals can cultivate a deeper connection with themselves, challenge traditional gender roles, and prioritize their mental, emotional, and physical well-being.

Cultivating Vitality and Well-being through Celibacy

Celibacy is often misunderstood and associated with religious vows, but it can be a powerful tool for cultivating vitality and well-being in our lives. In this subchapter, we will explore the various ways in which celibacy can benefit individuals seeking spiritual enlightenment, personal growth, self-discipline, and more.

For Catholics, celibacy has traditionally been embraced by priests and nuns as a way to devote themselves fully to God. However, celibacy can also be a personal choice for individuals seeking a deeper connection with themselves and the world around them. By abstaining from sexual relationships, one can redirect their energy and focus towards personal goals, career aspirations, and mental and emotional well-being.

In a society that often pressures individuals to conform to societal expectations of relationships, celibacy can be a form of activism. By choosing celibacy, individuals challenge traditional gender roles and expectations, promoting a more inclusive and open-minded perspective on intimacy and relationships. It allows individuals to rebel against the societal pressure to be in a relationship, instead prioritizing their own personal growth and self-discovery.

Celibacy can also be a means to cultivate a deeper connection with oneself. By abstaining from sexual relationships, individuals can explore alternative forms of intimacy and relationships, such as cultivating platonic friendships, engaging in spiritual practices, and focusing on self-care. This intentional solitude allows for introspection and self-reflection, fostering personal growth, and a stronger sense of self.

Moreover, celibacy can be a means of preserving personal energy and vitality. Sexual energy is often seen as a potent life force, and by abstaining from sexual activity, individuals can redirect this energy towards personal goals, creativity, and spiritual practices. This preservation of energy can lead to increased vitality, focus, and a sense of purpose.

In conclusion, celibacy can be a powerful tool for individuals seeking spiritual enlightenment, personal growth, self-discipline, and well-being. By embracing celibacy, Catholics, and individuals from various niches can challenge societal expectations, prioritize their mental and emotional well-being, cultivate a deeper connection with oneself, explore alternative forms of intimacy, and preserve personal energy and vitality. Embracing celibacy for these purposes can lead to a more fulfilling and purposeful life, grounded in self-discovery and personal growth.